How Earth Tells Us Its Age

Monika Davies

Consultants

Benjamin Andrews
Geologist and Associate Curator of Rocks and Ores
National Museum of Natural History

Cheryl Lane, M.Ed.
Seventh Grade Science Teacher
Chino Valley Unified School District

Michelle Wertman, M.S.Ed.
Literacy Specialist
New York City Public Schools

Publishing Credits

Rachelle Cracchiolo, M.S.Ed., *Publisher*
Emily R. Smith, M.A.Ed., *SVP of Content Development*
Véronique Bos, *VP of Creative*
Dani Neiley, *Editor*
Fabiola Sepulveda, *Art Director*

Smithsonian Enterprises

Avery Naughton, *Licensing Coordinator*
Paige Towler, *Editorial Lead*
Jill Corcoran, *Senior Director, Licensed Publishing*
Brigid Ferraro, *Vice President of New Business and Licensing*
Carol LeBlanc, *President*

Image Credits: cover: NASA ID:16611703184; p.7, 10, 11, 13, 20, 21, 24, 32 USGS; p.14 Emmanuel Douzery; p.15 Robert M. Lavinsky; p.25 Metropolitan Museum of Art; all other images from iStock and/or Shutterstock or in the public domain

Library of Congress Cataloging in Publication Control Number:
2024039529

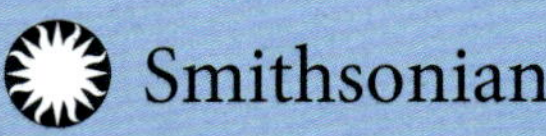

5482 Argosy Avenue
Huntington Beach, CA 92649
www.tcmpub.com
ISBN 979-8-7659-6892-5

Printed by: 51497
Printed in: China

Table of Contents

Our Mysterious Planet

Are we alone in the universe, or is there life beyond our solar system? How did life begin, and exactly how many species call Earth home? For centuries, humans have grappled with **existential** questions like these. Humans are naturally curious creatures. We love to contemplate and ponder questions that seem unanswerable at first. We have dedicated countless time to one question in particular: How old is planet Earth?

This hasn't been an easy mystery to solve. That's because much of Earth's origin story remains uncertain. Scientists know that Earth formed out of a collision of stardust and gas that circled our sun. However, Earth cannot give us its birth certificate. Scientists do not have a neat stack of written records to piece together an exact time line of early events. Yet over the years, scientists have discovered some answers about Earth's earliest days.

Today, scientists widely agree that Earth is about 4.54 billion years old—plus or minus about 50 million years. But, how did scientists figure out the age of Earth? Experts throughout the last century have tugged on their detective hats and looked at the clues Earth left us. Rocks, Earth's layers, and tree growth rings are the three ways that Earth tells us its age. We just have to study and observe them closely.

Rocks like this one are found all over Earth.

The trunks of all trees have visible growth rings.

Earth

FUN FACT

Lord Kelvin was a British mathematician. In 1862, he guessed that Earth was about 20 to 400 million years old. His estimate was very low. Scientists today know that Earth is much older than that!

Clue 1: Investigate the Rocks

What items across the planet hold the biggest clues to Earth's age? One might first think that mountain ranges or vast forests would have the most tales to tell about Earth. However, a range of ordinary, hard materials holds the most clues to Earth's age—rocks!

Rocks come in all shapes and sizes, and they are found across the planet. Investigating the structure of rocks helps scientists learn about Earth and its history.

Wadi Rum Desert in Jordan

Garden of the Gods in Colorado

Rocks of Suesca in Colombia

Scientists examine igneous rocks.

The Rock Cycle

Rocks are the oldest objects on the planet. Some rocks on Earth are billions of years old. Scientists have different ways to discover the ages of rocks.

Rocks go through a life cycle, and understanding how rocks form and change is a key part of knowing how to find their ages. Scientists date minerals in rocks, which means figuring out their exact ages or how they fit into a time line of events. When scientists can pinpoint the age of a rock, they can use this information to develop a time line of Earth's earliest days.

While rocks offer useful clues to Earth's age, they do have some drawbacks. Rocks do not stay the same over their lifetimes because they often go through the rock cycle. In this cycle, rocks form, fall apart, change appearances, and re-form as other types of rocks. These changes can take thousands of years. Sometimes, they can even take millions, or hundreds of millions, of years!

Three Types of Rocks

Three main types of rocks circle through the rock cycle. Different processes help form, break down, and change rocks.

Igneous rocks start as magma, which is hot, molten, liquid rock tucked under Earth's surface. Magma might creep up through cracks in the planet's surface or erupt from a volcano. As magma cools on Earth's surface, it transforms into igneous rocks.

Sedimentary rocks are a creative **mosaic**. Over long periods of time, wind and water wear away at existing rocks. This process is known as **erosion**. Tiny bits of rocks, sand, and other materials get squeezed and solidified together. The result is sedimentary rocks, which form in layers. The bottom layers are older than the top layers.

Metamorphic rocks are rocks that have transformed from the other two types. In other words, metamorphic rocks were once igneous or sedimentary rocks. Sometimes, metamorphic rocks can change into new forms of metamorphic rocks! These rocks form in places where tectonic plates, or large sections of Earth's outer layer, collide. When two plates crash together, some of the rocks are forced deep into the ground, increasing temperature and pressure. This creates the perfect conditions for metamorphic rocks to form.

SCIENCE

Fossil Finds

Fossils contain rich details of life from long ago. Fossils are the preserved remains of ancient plants and animals. Leaves, skeletons, animal footprints, and even eggs can turn into fossils. The majority of fossils are found in sedimentary rocks.

Archaeopteryx fossil in sedimentary rock

The Rock Cycle

Relative and Absolute Dating

Discovering the ages of different rocks helps **geologists** build a time line of Earth's history. Rock dating comes in two forms: relative and absolute. Each form relies on different methods.

A geologist examines thin layers of volcanic ash between other sediment layers.

Relative dating occurs when scientists take two rocks and compare them side-by-side. Scientists examine them to find which rock is older and has been on the planet longer.

One example of this type of dating is **stratigraphy**. This practice mainly looks at sedimentary rocks. In sedimentary rocks, the lowest layers are formed first. These are the oldest layers. Meanwhile, the highest layers are the most recently formed, meaning they are the youngest. When scientists compare these layers, they can get an idea of the relative age of each layer. This allows them to piece together a time line of past events. For example, if a fossil is found in a lower layer, they know that fossil is older than another fossil found in a higher layer.

Relative dating does not give scientists exact ages for rocks or for Earth. However, when it was first used, it gave scientists early hints that Earth was billions of years old rather than millions. That's because there were so many layers of rock and different groupings of fossils. Scientists realized that more time must have passed for there to be so many different types of fossils.

Geological Engineering

Geological engineering pairs Earth science with engineering. Many engineering projects require a knowledge of Earth's surface and structure. Geological engineers work to understand the history of Earth and how it has changed. This knowledge allows them to better direct engineering projects.

geological engineers

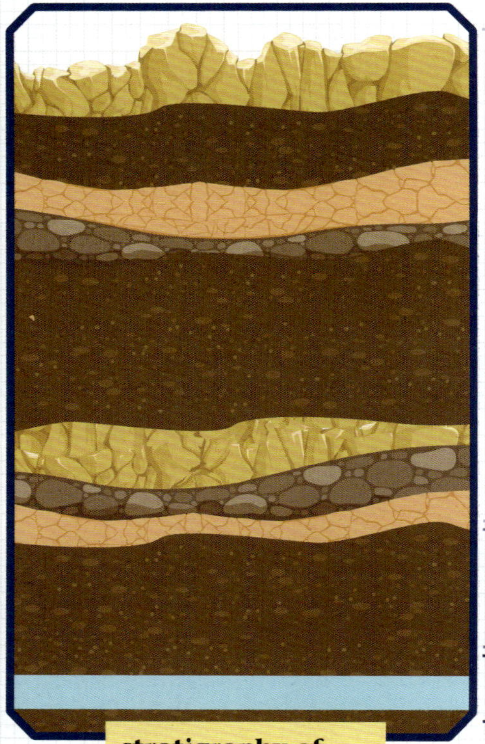

 limestone

 shale

 sandstone

 composite rock

 Colorado River

stratigraphy of the Grand Canyon

Geologists are often curious about *why* and *how* past events occurred. Once they know *when* an event happened, the *why* and *how* become easier to piece together. This is where absolute dating comes in. Absolute dating is a more exact process than relative dating. It can provide the exact age of a rock by measuring a rock's physical properties.

Radiometric dating is the main method of absolute dating. This process examines **radioactive** elements that make up certain rocks. It looks at the decay, or slow breakdown, of these elements. During decay, these elements break down and release energy. The time it takes for an element to break down is precise. This timing is called a *half-life*. It is the exact number of years it takes for half of the radioactive element to break down. Scientists know the half-lives of all radioactive elements. They commonly use potassium and uranium in this method. That's because these elements take a long time to decay, so they can be used to measure long periods of time.

To find the age of a rock, scientists measure the amounts of the radioactive element and the element to which it decays that are present in the rock. To do this, they look at the numbers of **particles** in the **nucleus**. The **ratio** of those two measurements provides a precise age date for the rock.

Scientists use technology like this machine to measure ratios in radiometric dating.

A geologist collects a fossil sample for radiometric dating.

MATHEMATICS

Radiocarbon Dating

Absolute dating can be used to find the ages of once-living plants and animals. To do this, scientists measure the amount of remaining **carbon-14**. This method can be used to date organisms between 50 and 50,000 years old.

coral skeletons used for radiocarbon dating

Ancient Rocks and Crystals

Earth's oldest rock is called the *Acasta Gneiss*. This rock was formed around 4.03 billion years ago! The Acasta Gneiss is in a **continental shield**. It is a part of Earth's crust that contains rocks that are extremely old.

To determine this rock's age, scientists studied crystals in the rock. Zircon, a mineral, made up the crystals in the rock. Zircon's radioactive element is uranium. Scientists were able to measure how much uranium was still in the rock to find its age. Since uranium has a half-life of 4.5 billion years, it was a reliable element to measure.

The Acasta Gneiss was found north of the city of Yellowknife in Canada.

While the Acasta Gneiss is the oldest rock on the planet, scientists have found even older crystals. Zircon crystals dated to 4.4 billion years ago were found in western Australia. It's possible that there are even older crystals—and rocks—on Earth. But the rock cycle makes it hard to know for sure. This cycle changes and re-forms rocks, so it's possible that older rocks may have been destroyed.

Still, proof of ancient rocks and crystals are dotted across the planet's continents. Each one has stood the test of time and been through the planet's many changes. Knowing their ages has helped scientists confirm their estimates that Earth is billions of years old.

zircon crystals

Astronaut Harrison Schmitt collects lunar rock samples in 1972.

FUN FACT

Astronauts brought samples of moon rocks back to Earth. Scientists were able to date them. The oldest sample from the moon was about 4.5 million years old. It was a piece of the moon's crust.

Clue 2:
Explore Earth's Layers

Earth is a planet with active tectonic plates. It has a surface that's always on the move. The theory of **plate tectonics** gives shape, understanding, and backstory to Earth's time line. And, plate tectonics explains the layers of Earth, which is our next clue. We can get fresh insights into Earth's age and history by exploring the planet's layers.

Erta Ale volcano in Ethiopia

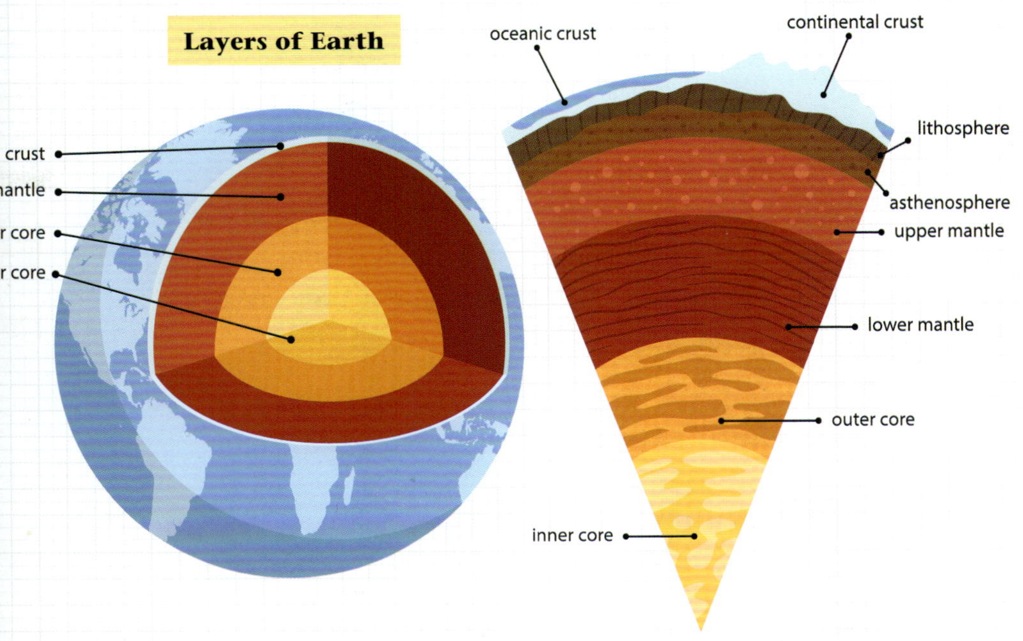

Three Layers

Earth is more than its surface of land and oceans. It also has a hidden depth that humans have barely explored. There are three main layers to Earth's underground structure: the crust, the mantle, and the core.

First, Earth's top layer is the crust. This thin outer layer of rock forms Earth's surface. There are two types of crust: oceanic crust and continental crust. Oceanic crust is beneath the oceans. Continental crust is generally older, thicker, and forms the continents. Next, the mantle is located below the crust. It is mostly made of solid minerals, but it flows and moves over hundreds of years. It is Earth's thickest layer. Last, Earth's core sits below the mantle at the center of the planet. It is made of scorching-hot metal, and it is the hottest part of our planet.

Earth's crust hovers and floats on top of the mantle. The crust is made of tectonic plates that move and shift, helping scientists learn about Earth's age and history.

A Puzzle of Plates

Plate tectonics is the theory that Earth's crust is made of giant plates, or slabs of rock, that move. Plates sit on top of Earth's mantle, moving at a very slow pace. Most plates only move about 5–10 centimeters (2–4 inches) a year. There are seven major plates, as well as eight minor ones. The plates curve with the planet. The places where they meet are called *plate boundaries.*

Plate boundaries are important because this is where the most action happens. At boundary lines, plates rub and collide with each other. This movement can pull rocks down under Earth's surface. It can also lead to the formation of new metamorphic rocks. And when two plates slide up against each other, these new rocks can be slowly pushed upward to form mountain ranges. This process takes a very long time—millions to hundreds of millions of years!

Plate Tectonics

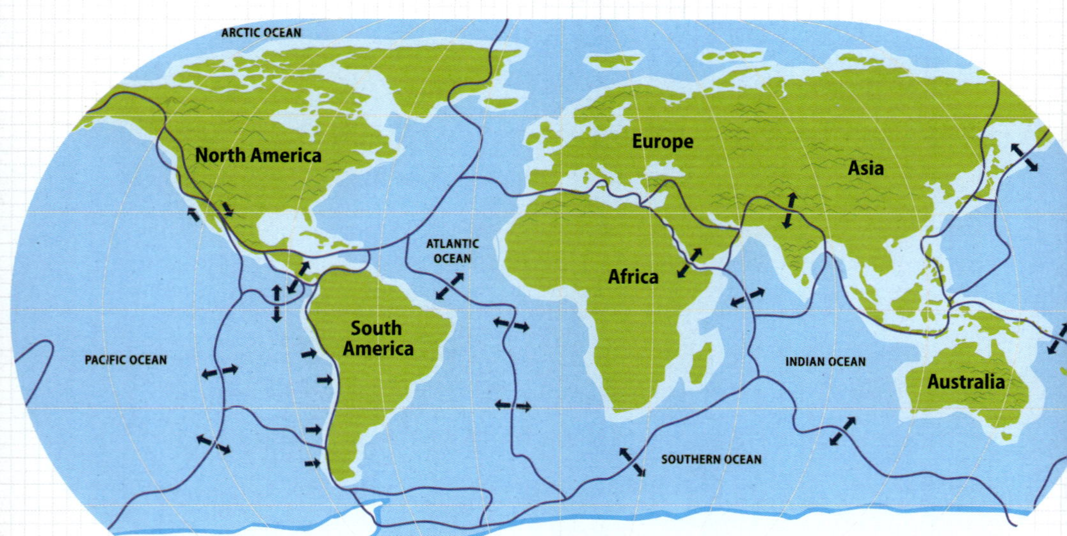

These lines and arrows show plate boundaries and movement.

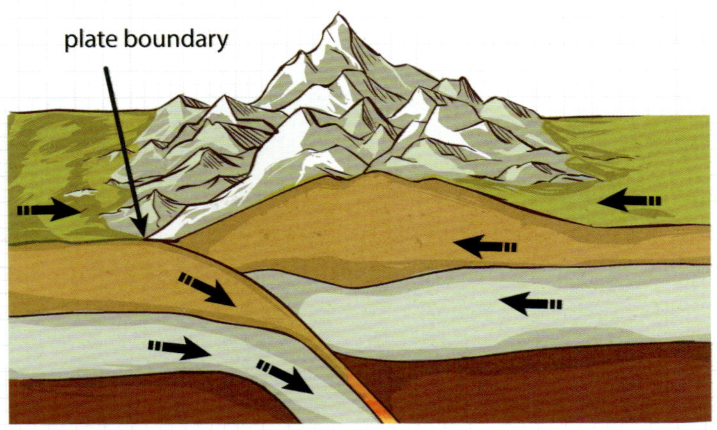

Understanding plate tectonics gives scientists a more complete picture of Earth's history. By studying plates, scientists have learned that mountains that stand tall now were once just flat surfaces of land. Continents that are now thousands of kilometers apart were once joined together. Earth's surface looked very different billions of years ago.

The rocks that make up the Dolomite Mountains in Italy formed at the bottom of an ocean about 250 million years ago.

This fissure, or crack in the ground, formed in Iceland as a result of tectonic plate movement.

Ocean Layers

Scientists have been able to find the ages of continental crust and oceanic crust. They used the same dating methods as they do for rocks. Continental crust is the older of the two, and some pieces have been dated to billions of years old. Meanwhile, oceanic crust is younger. It has been dated to about 200 million years old.

On average, oceanic crust measures around 6 kilometers (4 miles) in depth. Here, layers of sediment give clues as to changing ocean conditions. Sediment ranges from dust and dirt to **plankton** shells. The top layers showcase the ocean's recent history. But deeper layers tell of the more distant past.

A scientist examines an ocean sediment core sample.

TECHNOLOGY

Deep-Sea Drilling

Scientists use a special tool called a *corer* to take sediment samples. Corers come in many shapes and forms to **extract** samples. For example, a piston corer uses a long tube to nosedive into sediment. It can then pull out a long sample measuring up to 27 meters (90 feet) in length!

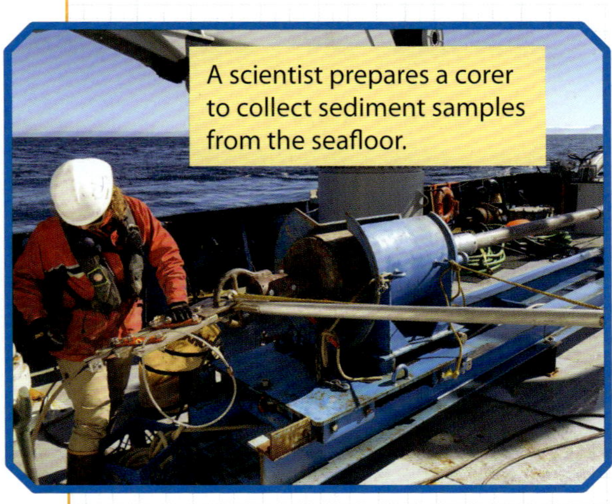

A scientist prepares a corer to collect sediment samples from the seafloor.

Scientists use special tools to pull up samples of sea sediments. These samples form cylinders that show different layers. Some samples show a dramatic shift from light to dark sediments. This color change gives scientists a clue about historical events. Millions of years ago, the atmosphere had an increase in carbon dioxide. This gas made air temperatures rise, and the ocean absorbed a lot of that gas, too. This gas changed the ocean's structure. It also affected the organisms that lived in the ocean. They had less oxygen in the water, and scientists discovered that there was a **mass extinction**. This part of the ocean's story is reflected in the color change of sediment layers.

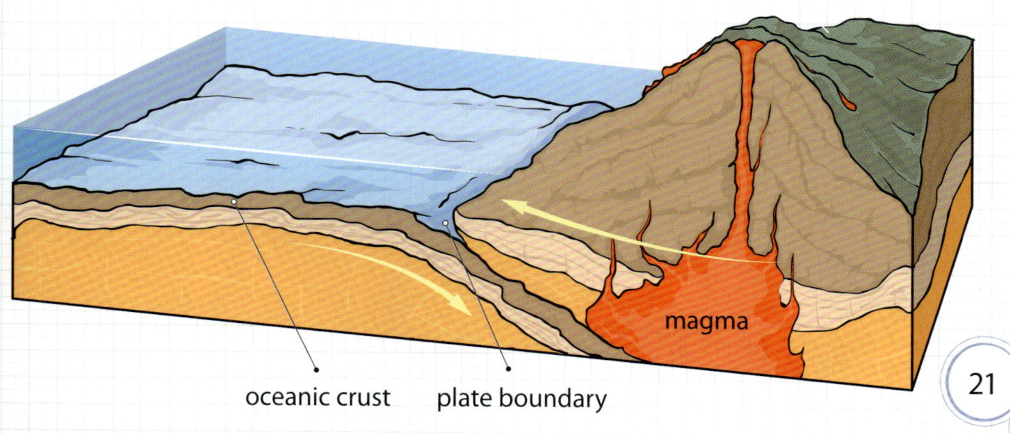

Clue 3: Analyze the Rings

Rocks and Earth's layers provide strong clues as to Earth's age. But some living organisms—trees—hold clues to historical events and climate history. Trees can live for hundreds, and sometimes even thousands, of years. Trees have longer lifespans than most plant and animal species, and they also carry stories in their trunks. These giant organisms help scientists learn more about the past 5,000 years on Earth, the same span of time as recorded human history.

Giant sequoias can live for more than 3,000 years.

world's oldest living tree

FUN FACT

A bristlecone pine tree in California holds the title of the world's oldest living tree. Experts took samples of the core of the tree to find its age. The samples show that it is at least 4,855 years old!

Cutting a tree trunk exposes all the growth rings inside.

A Grove of Tales

When you look at a **cross section** of a tree trunk, you'll notice that the wood has a pattern of rings. The trunk of every tree contains rings that each tell a story. Every year, a tree widens as it grows, and this growth is marked with a growth ring. Growth rings are indicated with light layers and dark layers in the wood. Light layers, which are thicker, take shape in warmer times and mark a growing season. Dark layers are thinner and develop as the weather cools. These layers signify when trees begin to slow their growth.

Finding the age of a tree involves counting the growth rings inside the trunk. One dark ring and one light ring equals one year. The science of dating growth rings is called *dendrochronology*. "Dendro" comes from a Greek work that means "tree," and chronology is a science that measures time and dates events.

A Chronicle of Climate

Trees experience many seasons throughout their lifetimes. In their growth rings, scientists can find clues that point to past **droughts**, forest fires, and rainy years. When scientists put all this information together, a time line of the area's climate emerges.

Trees do not need to fall or be cut down to reveal this information. Instead, scientists use a tool called an *increment borer* to take samples of a tree. This tool can twirl and cut into a tree, pulling out a straw-like slice of wood **tissue**. Taking tissue samples in this way does not harm trees. It allows scientists to discover what trees in an environment have experienced.

A scientist uses an increment borer to take a sample from a tree and study its growth.

Most places on Earth only have around a few hundred years or less of recorded climate data. But trees host much longer time lines in their trunks. For example, a scar in place of a growth ring can show that a tree experienced a forest fire at some point in time. A small, dark growth ring can show that a tree experienced a drought. Scientists can use that data to determine whether the people who lived in that area moved to other areas as a result. That's because climate has always had a big impact on where and how humans choose to live. Trees can give data points that inform scientists' understanding of human movements and history.

ARTS

The Art of Dendrochronology

Many old European paintings use oak panels as backdrops. People have used dendrochronology to figure out the ages of these paintings. As long as the panels are made of oak, they can be dated. Other types of wood are harder to date accurately.

oak panel painting

An Old-Timer

Earth has been spinning in our universe for over 4.5 billion years. The planet has billions of years of stories tucked away in rocks, layers, and trees. Scientists have excavated and dated some of the information these sources provide. However, it will take many more years for us to puzzle through them all. Across the planet, there are vast, unmapped areas. There are thick stretches of the Amazon Rainforest that we have barely explored. And the majority of our oceans remain a murky mystery.

Understanding our past informs our future. Knowing Earth's age and history gives us perspective on how long our planet has been here. This knowledge also shows us how it has transformed. Plus, **climate change** will continue to shift our seasons and maps. It's worthwhile to understand how Earth's climate story has developed over billions of years.

Earth has left us clues to millions of untold stories. We glimpse the tales in old (and new) rocks, layers of Earth, and the light and dark rings within trees. Every story has chapters rich with details, which is also true for Earth's age and time line. What remains to be seen is what stories we will discover next about our ancient—and changing—planet Earth.

STEAM CHALLENGE

Define the Problem

Geologists are working to demonstrate how rocks are cycled over time. They are seeking models to display in various museums of natural history throughout the country. The exhibit will be called "Mock Rocks" and will include the most accurate models you and other groups can create.

Constraints: You may only use the materials supplied to you.

Criteria: You will create three models that begin as one type of rock. Your models should be able to fit into the palm of your hand and should clearly model three distinct types of rocks (igneous, metamorphic, and sedimentary).

Research and Brainstorm

What is sediment, and what does it have to do with rock formation? How are Earth's materials cycled through the planet? What force propels the cycling of Earth's materials? What elements must be present for the three types of rocks to form?

Design and Build

Draw a model to show how each type of rock is formed. Label each phase with how you will manipulate your materials to create the three different rock types. Collect the materials you will need for your rock cycle journey.

Test and Improve

Break, smash, melt, mold, or shave your materials to create your first type of rock. If you are successful, break off a piece. Then, using the remainder of the first rock, follow your plan to create the second type of rock. If you are successful, break off another piece. Finally, use the remainder of the second rock to create the third type of rock. Once you have completed testing, look at your three rocks. What changes can you make to create more accurate models for one or all the rock types? Make adjustments to your plan and test again.

Reflect and Share

What did you enjoy about this challenge? What part did you and your group find most difficult? What characteristics do your model rocks have in common with real rocks? How can studying rocks help us understand the age of our planet?

Glossary

carbon-14—a distinct isotope of the element carbon that is used in radiocarbon dating

climate change—long-term shifts in temperatures and weather patterns on Earth

continental shield—large areas of Earth's crust that are made of crystalline rocks and are rarely changed by the movement of tectonic plates

cross section—a cutting that exposes the interior of something

droughts—extended periods of time where there is very little to no rain

erosion—the gradual wearing away of soil, rock, or land by natural forces including water, wind, or ice

existential—relating to the meaning, purpose, and value of human existence

extract—to remove something

geologists—scientists who study the history of Earth and its life, especially as recorded in rocks

mass extinction—an event in which many living species on Earth experience rapid extinction rates during a relatively short period of time

mosaic—something made up of many different things

nucleus—the central core of an atom, which contains protons and neutrons

particles—basic units of matter and energy, such as atoms, protons, neutrons, or electrons

plankton—tiny animal and plant life in oceans, lakes, and other bodies of water

plate tectonics—a theory in geology that Earth's crust is divided into moving plates whose movements cause activity such as earthquakes

radioactive—giving off energy as a result of the decay of atoms

ratio—the relationship in quantity, amount, or size between two or more things

stratigraphy—a branch of geology that involves the study of strata, or rock layers

tissue—cellular material that forms parts in humans, animals, and plants

Index

CAREER ADVICE
from Smithsonian

Do you want to be a geologist?

Here are some tips to keep in mind for the future.

"Look closely at the rocks around you and think about how they formed. Each one tells part of Earth's story."

*– **Benjamin Andrews,** Geologist, National Museum of Natural History*

"Next time you take a trip—across town or across the world—look around at the land. Do you see volcanoes? A river delta? A large lake? Try to learn when and how the landforms you see developed, and begin your journey into Earth's past."

*– **Elizabeth Cottrell,** Geologist and Chair of the Department of Mineral Sciences, National Museum of Natural History*